S0-BAX-261

Introduction

From a very young age, children make magical connections with books. From listening to favorite stories read aloud to simply turning the pages and identifying familiar objects through pictures, very young children explore and enjoy the wonder of books. As children are immersed in a variety of book experiences, they inevitably grow curious about the sounds they hear and the words they see. This connection between the letters of the alphabet and the sounds each letter makes, known as phonemic awareness, is a very important prerequisite skill for learning to read. Phonemic awareness is an essential first step in reading readiness because children need to be able to hear and manipulate oral sound patterns before they can relate them to print.

Now I'm Reading!™ *All About the ABCs* Pre-Reader for emergent readers is just right for children who are beginning to recognize the letters of the alphabet and identify the sounds they make. Each spread focuses on a different letter of the alphabet and its sound. The patterned, repetitive text and the simple yet bold illustrations encourage very young children to "read" the pictures while also recognizing letters and sounds. The goal of the Now I'm Reading™ series is to encourage a love of reading by providing opportunities for early reading success. These emergent books are the best way to start your child on the road to being a lifelong reader.

Apes

Apes and alligators

Apes and alligators
and an airplane

Apes and alligators and
an airplane on an
alphabet adventure

Balls

Balls and bears

Balls and bears and
bubbles

Balls and bears and
bubbles in the bath

Cats

Cats and crowns

Cats and crowns and camels

Cats and crowns and camels going to a castle

Dogs

Dogs and ducks

Dogs and ducks and
donkeys

Dogs and ducks and
donkeys wearing diapers

ALL ABOUT

E

Eagles

Eagles and emus

Eagles and emus and
an elephant

Eagles and emus
and an elephant
exercising

Foxes

Foxes and frogs

Foxes and frogs and
flamingos

Foxes and frogs and
flamingos with fleas

Goats

Goats and a gorilla

Goats and a gorilla and
geese

Goats and a gorilla and
geese seeing a ghost

Hens

Hens and hamsters

Hens and hamsters and horses

Hens and hamsters and horses rolling down a hill

ALL ABOUT

I

Inchworms

Inchworms and iguanas

Inchworms and iguanas
and ice cream

Inchworms and iguanas
and ice cream on an
island

ALL ABOUT

J

Jewels

Jewels and jugglers

Jewels and jugglers and a jaguar

Jewels and jugglers and a jaguar in the jungle

ALL ABOUT

K

Koalas

Koalas and kittens

Koalas and kittens and
kangaroos

Koalas and kittens and
kangaroos
in kindergarten

Lions

Lions and lambs

Lions and lambs and a
ladder

Lions and lambs and a
ladder in a lake

ALL ABOUT

M

Monkeys

Monkeys and masks

Monkeys and masks
and maps

Monkeys and masks
and maps on the moon

Newts

Newts and noodles

Newts and noodles
and nuts

Newts and noodles and
nuts needing a nurse

ALL ABOUT

O

Olives

Olives and overalls

Olives and overalls
and an octopus

Olives and overalls and
an octopus falling into
the ocean

Penguins

Penguins and parachutes

Penguins and
parachutes and
pizza

Penguins and
parachutes and
pizza at a party

ALL ABOUT

Q

Quails

Quails and queens

Quails and queens
with quilts

Quails and queens
with quilts
listening to a quartet

Rabbits

Rabbits and raccoons

Rabbits and raccoons
and roller skates

Rabbits and raccoons
and roller skates
in a race

Squirrels

Squirrels and skunks

Squirrels and skunks
and a sled

Squirrels and skunks
and a sled
stuck in the snow

Tents

Tents and tigers

Tents and tigers and
towels

Tents and tigers and
towels talking
on telephones

ALL ABOUT

U

Unicorns

Unicorns and uniforms

Unicorns and uniforms
and an umpire

Unicorns and uniforms
and an umpire in his
underwear

ALL ABOUT

V

Voles

Voles and violets

Voles and violets and a violin

Voles and violets
and a violin
on Valentine's Day

Wigs

Wigs and walruses

Wigs and walruses
and waves

Wigs and walruses
and waves
on a whale

ALL ABOUT

X

Oxen

Oxen and boxes

Oxen and boxes
and foxes

Oxen and boxes
and foxes
examining X-rays

ALL ABOUT

Y

Yaks

Yaks and yo-yos

Yaks and yo-yos
and yarn

Yaks and yo-yos and
yarn on a yacht

ALL ABOUT

Z

Zebras

Zebras and zippers

Zebras and zippers
and a zoo

Zebras and zippers and
a zoo . . . Zzzzzzzz

Extra Activities

Molding the Alphabet

Help your child form letters out of dough or modeling clay. Then, have your child close his or her eyes, feel a letter, and try to identify it by its shape. For a tasty modification of this activity, use alphabet cookie cutters to form and bake letter cookies. Then, your child can identify each letter before he or she eats it!

Letters in Nature

Take a walk outside to gather sticks or twigs with your child. Then, use the sticks to write different letters of the alphabet in the sand or dirt. As you are writing each letter, say the sound the letter makes, and ask your child to repeat the sound.

A Bendable Alphabet

Invite your child to use bendable objects, such as twist ties, cooked spaghetti, yarn, or pipe cleaners, to form the letters of the alphabet. Each time you or your child creates and names a letter, challenge him or her to say the letter's sound and think of an object that begins with that letter.

Shopping for Letters

On your next trip to the grocery store, help your child find and identify the letters of the alphabet all around the store. Encourage your child to point out the different letters on products and signs. Then say the name of the item for your child so that he or she hears the sound in the spoken word.

Disappearing Alphabet

This is a fun way to practice recognizing the letters of the alphabet while also trying to identify the sounds each letter makes. Using a small chalkboard and a wet sponge, write a letter on the chalkboard with the wet sponge. Then, encourage your child to say the name of the letter and its sound before the letter disappears!

Hide-and-Seek Alphabet

Write each letter of the alphabet on an index card or a small piece of paper. Next, while your child is not looking, hide the alphabet cards around the house. Then, have your child try to find each letter that is hidden in the house. As your child finds a letter, encourage him or her to say its name, say its sound, and come up with a word that begins with that letter.

Letter Patterns

This is a great activity for reinforcing letter recognition. Help your child use alphabet stamps (or cut out small paper squares and write each letter on at least six squares) to create letter patterns (for example, BCBCBC or ZYXZYXZYX) on a long strip of paper. After creating a pattern, encourage your child to "read" the pattern back to you.

Tactile Alphabet Book

This is an ongoing project that should take a few weeks to complete. Start by cutting a large block letter out of colored paper for each letter of the alphabet. Glue each letter onto a separate piece of white paper. Then, collect one item that represents each letter's beginning sound to glue on to the white paper with the corresponding letter. (For example, acorns for A, buttons for B, cotton balls for C, etc.) Next, introduce one letter page at a time to your child and discuss the item you'll be gluing on. Encourage your child to chant "A is for acorns" as he or she glues on the acorns, etc. After your child completes each page, bind the pages together to make a tactile alphabet book. By using his or her sense of touch and manipulating each item, your child will make a strong association between the letters and the sounds.

Messy Letters

Your child will have a blast practicing writing the letters of the alphabet using shaving cream. First, cover a table with a plastic tablecloth. Next, spread shaving cream on the tabletop. Then, show your child how to use his or her fingers to write the letters of the alphabet in the shaving cream. You can also say a letter sound or name an object and have your child write the corresponding letter in the shaving cream. (Note: Be sure to warn your child not to put any shaving cream in his or her eyes or mouth.)

Letters After Dark

Write each letter of the alphabet on an index card or a piece of paper. Hang the cards on the walls of a room in your home. Then, after dark, turn out the lights, and have your child shine a flashlight around the room to find and identify each letter of the alphabet.

Mystery Bag

Collect twenty-six objects, each one beginning with a different letter of the alphabet. Place the objects in a special "mystery" bag. Have your child close his or her eyes, reach into the bag, and pull out an object. Then, encourage your child to name the object and say the letter it starts with!

Eating the Alphabet

Use small pieces of food, such as cereal, pretzels, or berries, to form the letters of the alphabet on a paper plate. Then, invite your child to identify and eat the letters you have made!

Letter Detective

In this activity, choose one letter to focus on for about one week. Begin this activity by giving your child a small jar with a lid. Label the jar with the letter you will be focusing on. Then, each time your child spots the specific letter—around town, in a book, or on television—allow him or her to add a penny to the jar. After one week, open the jar, and have your child count the pennies.

Catch That Sound

Choose a letter of the alphabet, and find a bouncy ball to throw. To play this game, toss the ball back and forth with your child. Each time you or your child throws the ball, name an item that begins with that letter. See how many times you can throw the ball while saying a word that begins with your letter—before running out of words!

Chant That Name

Do this activity to help your child practice blending the different sounds in a given word (or name). Say the following chant:

> It starts with "T"
> And it ends with "om."
> Put them together
> And they say _____. (Tom)

Use your child's name first. Then use the names of friends and family members!

Paper Plate Puzzles

Print an uppercase letter on the left side of a paper plate and the corresponding lowercase letter on the right. Cut each paper plate into two parts with a zigzag or wavy line to make two puzzle pieces. Mix all the puzzle pieces, and have your child put them together again. (This could also be done by writing a letter on one half of the plate and drawing or gluing a picture that begins with that letter sound on the other half of the plate.)

Write On

Make letter-writing fun for your child by having him or her practice writing letters with a variety of interesting tools and materials, such as chalk on a chalkboard, wipe-off markers on a whiteboard, magic slates, finger paint, watercolors, etc. You could also have fun with alphabet stencils!

Alphabet Hang-up

Write the letters of the alphabet onto twenty-six wooden clothespins. Then, together with your child, cut out magazine pictures, one for each letter of the alphabet, and have your child match the clothespin letters to the beginning sounds of the magazine pictures. Clip the clothespins to the corresponding pictures.

Dot-to-Dot Alphabet

Practice letter recognition and alphabetical order with this hands-on activity. First, draw a dot-to-dot outline of a simple picture. (Try tracing pictures from old coloring books.) Then, starting with the letter A, place each letter of the alphabet at a consecutive dot. Have your child connect the dots by identifying each letter!

Rhyme-Time Rhythm

Explain to your child that you are going to say three rhyming words, such as *cat, hat, bat.* Then, have your child extend the rhyme by suggesting other words that rhyme with those three, for example, *pat, mat, rat.* Or, as a variation to this activity, say three words to your child, such as *pin, tin, sit,* and have your child tell you which word does not rhyme with the others.

Musical Syllables

Help your child hear the distinct syllables in a given word by adding a musical touch. Using drums, a piano, a xylophone, or any other musical instrument, or simply by clapping your hands, "play aloud" the syllables in the given word. For example, first say the word "sandwich" to your child. Then, have your child clap or play the two distinct beats (or syllables) in that word.

Simon Says Alphabet

Write each letter of the alphabet on an index card or small piece of paper. Have your child spread out the alphabet cards in front of him or her on the floor. Proceed with a rollicking game of Simon Says by using such commands as "Simon says touch the letter E with your thumb," "Simon says pick up the letter that makes the 'D' sound," "Simon says turn over the letters O and V," etc.

Thumbs Up for Sounds

Give your child a smiley sticker to stick on his or her thumb. Next, choose a specific letter sound, such as "P." Then, tell your child to give a smiling thumbs-up signal each time he or she hears the "P" sound at the beginning of a word. Begin by reading or saying a list of words, some that have the "P" sound at the beginning and some that do not. As a challenging variation on this activity, have your child signal middle or ending sounds with a thumbs-up.

Taste Experiences A to Z

Over the course of many weeks, introduce your child to a variety of taste experiences related to the letters of the alphabet. By using his or her sense of taste while hearing food words, your child will make a meaningful association between each letter of the alphabet and its sound. Here are a few suggestions: A–apple, avocado, apricot; B–bagel, bologna, blueberry; C–caramel, cucumber, cantaloupe.

Name That Sound

Ask your child to listen to a set of three words. Then, encourage him or her to tell you what the first or last sound is in the set. For example, say, "You tell me what the last sound is in these words: *boot, foot, pet.*" (You can then ask your child to think of other words that end with the "T" sound.)

Alphabet Dictionary

This is a wonderful project that can be completed over time. Help your child print a letter of the alphabet on each page of a book put together from sheets of plain or colored paper. Then, have your child draw a picture of an object that begins with that letter to place on the corresponding page. You could also cut and paste magazine pictures or use appropriate stickers that correspond to each letter in this homemade dictionary.

Handwriting Practice

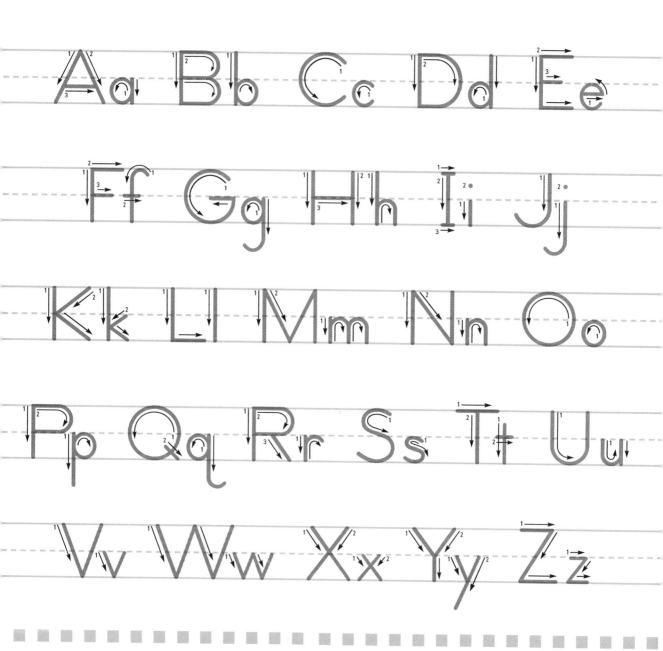

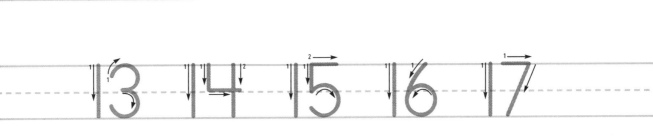

1 2 3 4 5 6

7 8 9 10 11 12

13 14 15 16 17

18 19 20

Letter Match

Using the letter stickers from the Parent Guide, match the letter to the picture that begins with that letter.

place
A
here

place
B
here

place
C
here

place
D
here

place
E
here

place
F
here

place
G
here

place
H
here

place
I
here

place
J
here

place
K
here

place
L
here

place
M
here

place
N
here

place
O
here

place
P
here

place
Q
here

place
R
here

place
S
here

place
T
here

place
U
here

place
V
here

place
W
here

place
X
here

place
Y
here

place
Z
here

NOTES